S0-BDW-832

the Dedalus Press

editor John F Deane

FLEURS-DU-LIT

by

TOM MAC INTYRE

DEDALUS

THE DEDALUS PRESS
24 The Heath, Cypress Downs, Dublin 6W

© Tom Mac Intyre 1990

ISBN 0 948268 83 2 (paper)
ISBN 0 948268 84 0 (bound)

Cover Design: The Graphiconies

Setting: Clíona Ní Bhréartúin

Printed in Ireland by Colour Books Ltd., Dublin

Acknowledgement is due to the editors of the following publications in which some of these poems originally appeared: "In Dublin", "The Irish Times", "Poetry Australia", "The Poetry Ireland Review", "Salmon", "The Honest Ulsterman", "The Irish Review", "The University Review", "Thirty-two Counties" (Secker & Warburg), "Tracks".

The Dedalus Press receives financial assistance from An Chomhairle Ealaíon, The Arts Council, Ireland.

CONTENTS

FOOTHOLD

This is the anchor
knows the tides

this is the snake
that never sleeps

this is the foot
that you brought back
to quiet the snake
that never sleeps

to sound the anchor
that knows the tides
to bless the snake
that never sleeps

to name the anchor

that knows the tides

FOR GERALDINE

KOINOS HERMES

HOME PLACE

Rime on the pane,
spittle-and-thumb,
spittle-and-thumb,
the glass clears,

snow on the lawn,
the trees, familiar
trees, night quiet
something else again,

the glass blurs,
spittle-and-thumb,
spittle-and-thumb,
the glass clears,

the snow, the lawn,
the trees dispose
inalienable quiet,

December gift
for December man,
spittle-and-thumb,
rime on the pane.

EUREKA

There's a buzz.

Sins bathe my lips.

I'm either cunt-struck,
I make confession
like the bee,
or CUNT-struck.

There's quite a buzz.

"Cunt-struck," that's
a-ching a-ching
a-ching a-ching
but "CUNT-struck" -
I gloss an ocean -
that's a-CHINNGGG...

I can't wait
to tell her
and I do

and oh how
uneasily she looks
me up and down
and down and up
and up and down.

SEASIDE

Ebb-tide: the fisherman's step
says — "Work done, the work begins",

he enters a shore-pool, spear-
stick poised, strikes twice, sets
the fish by the pool's edge —

I know you and I don't

when you surface again
in the choral last of the day,
sea-urchin, wishbone, tousled undine,

"But I'm explaining" — that's you, isn't it?
"I'm explaining" — isn't that you, love?

isn't it? isn't it?
isn't that you?

THE PURPLE FLOWER

The purple flower
sprig of a thing
finding a way

the purple yields
underplumage
first feathering's
indolent down

the purple frees
purple on fire
tourbillon deeps
fire the purple

the petals move
five to the flower
as one they move
pillow and fire
one in the weave

listen and hear
hear to the far
end of your bones

SUNNY JIM

becomes an ardent line,

his line becomes
la langue d'oiseaux,
the bird-man streams
hieroglyphic ABC —

Your two white feathers
where the fish long to be,

your Brian O'Linn,
your heifer of one spin,
your ass's heat,
your dove-grey horse,

your original bottle, your whirr,
your whizz in the thrapple, your
ould segotia, me ould segotia…

Au revoir, and out
the door in smoke.

AT THE ZOO

...we go down the slope
to the polar bears,

her soft-shoe shuffle,
swing of her brazen head,

humming like an oboe
he stands his ground,

adagio of sundown,

they know the circle,
tune the radii,

we linger in the rye
of behemoth and butterfly.

BIRTHDAY GIFT

December moon ushers
the black swan, serif
to the small hours —

clutch your brave pomander —

the swan's on course,
there's no stay tonight,

not a sound
in either world.

VAE VICTIS

Hungry for this
he took her
aboard, she straddled
the brave shoulders,
the two smiled,

"Are you alright?"
"Are *you* alright?"

He took off,
ran so fast
by the time
he stopped, nothing
left bar her
bare shinbones:

he fired them
into a lake,
took breath, turned
to face the life,

world learned
that honed thigh
and trophied breast,

never the hung
lip, dry mouth,
the mirror-shake
night or morning

until in her
own good time
she stirred, rose
from the lake,
the growthy pool,

scoured the land,
sniffed his road,
his open door —

"Are you alright?"
stuck in the jamb
extended a limb,
"Are you alright?"

dusk's sweetest milk
her revenant smile.

SKYLINE

Hunter well-weathered,
you with such flair
for the clean kill,
have you considered
cross number four
on your afternoon hill?

CANDOUR OF THE WELL

The table
set for one, the bowl —
your *fruits-de-terre* —

where berry stares
at candle-end,
and candle-end
gives back the stare.

PRESTISSIMO

Gram for gram
no wilder-looking
specimen abroad,

the hooked beak,
the orange eye,
that barred breast,

holding you down
those talons drive
the hard bargain,

"I'm heir-presumptive",
he's always told you,
"to your presumptions",

the beak whirrs,
knows it's not
for stirring tea
he has it,

eye fulsome now,
the breast — perpends,
"*Table d'hôte* or
à la carte?" "*Buffet*" —
did he hear you say?

you've got to like him,
see to his needs,

smile as he feeds
without bothering to kill.

ANDROMEDA MUSING

Mother came close —
I am something special,
good job Perseus
made it on time.

......

Always a sucker
for The Square of Pegasus,
nothing to lose
but your *tabula rasa*.

......

Welcome back, Orion,
you're not the worst,
chill-factor King
of The Winter Sky.

......

Far sou'-west —
how she shines —
far sou'-west
the lovely Venus, yard-light
over all the farms.

FLEUR-DU-LIT

Somewhere else the eagle
bred the whirlwind,

where we lay
the one-strand river
was midnight nurse
and dawn's delay,

we heard eels whistling
in the heaps of the deep,

we slept under
the sound of the tide
and the seagulls' feet.

SHAPER

"Curve your right arm —
that becomes me",

turn your back
she's in heat,
wears amber and coral,
bloodstones for luck,
swears by the book
of her own compilation,

"Curve your left arm" —

while you nod
she renders herself,
she's a nipple, she's
the top of a nipple
at rest in the dark,

you remember
you saw her once
touch the breast
of a woman you loved.

RECEIVING

Unleavened bread leavens
my well-travelled tongue.

Near the altar a spring.

Redwood, the hallowed spade
infers a lucent throne.

You'll know my step —

she departs for the fields,
mother of the plants,
daughter of the deep-dish leaves.

THROWN FROM HER HORSE

for Olivia

And yes, I would love
to see this new play
called "Snow White", for me
it was called "Snow White
and The Seven Dwarfs",
a cartoon from Disney's,

congratulations on your visit
to Russia, on your play
"The Great Hunger", thank-you
for calling to see me
in hospital, I have to
learn like a baby again,

I don't hear much of what
the journalists are writing
about *The Peacock's* new play,

in Crosshaven we don't have "The Irish Times",
just "The Examiner" and "Evening Echo",

I have to learn
like a baby again.

COLLATION

Mobile under the skin
there's a foreign body,

breast-bone for haven.
My tepid fingers prod —

Don't push me around,
I've roots for miles.

My fingers pay no heed.
They probe, chivvy, squeeze,

they force a wound.
No blood, no vertigo,

the wound's lips drop
a radish in my hand,

the wound's lips close,
how simple it was,

the root's in my hand,
the firm, fleshy, plangent root.

DANSE HORIZONTALE

I don't like
the mortuary whiff,

a private public place,

can't see his face,
we're *main-à-main*
et corps-à-corps,

it goes on,
louche minuet,
duplicitous pavan,

stops, my head
moored by his groin,

a turgid cock solicits,

the proprietor
(O mon capitaine)
dissolves the rink.

THE DWARF

Night clean as amber,
lakes a paternoster,
long past formalities
the dwarf's obsidian eye,

I know the question —
the bog's consenting tones,
waxy jet, violet brown,
lie-de-vin, charred blues,
I know the question
that your blood imbrues.

Misericord's his name.

I want arms
to embrace him.

Night to start an answer,
the bog bears him away,
night to start an answer,
your slope of the mountain,
lakes a paternoster.

REVEILLE

Yesterday she left,
this morning a dove
to my window :

the dove's first call —
this is not cooing —
nine beats, and again,
this is firm, ferruled,
listen to the pause,

the second call
repeats the first,

the third lifts a notch, boldly
turns on the phrase,
frees awl, frees rasp,
frees bevelled hauteur,

furl, and release,
ushers the prim coda —

no wingbeat, none
expected, I lie there,
dove come, dove gone.

THE WHISPERER

I will teach you
the space inside
the space beside her,

I'm the quick one,
the naked, the bold
bad unbiddable child,

we'll go by night,
we'll go the wet
paths of the sea,

learn the love-bite
of that truth-water.

BALAUSTRA

We embrace in the hall,
I shout to banish ghosts,

modestly she cups, kisses
the modest whorl, well-worn,
which starts the banister,

baluster, *balaustra,* blossom
slender above and full below
the banisters pursue — *Hey* —

we touch, embrace again — blossom

of the wild pomegranate,
apple with the grain.

LANDSCAPE

The eastern mountains
glimpse the sea,

and, climbers tell,
the western mountains
the greater sea,

the heartland plies
saucy shadow, secret
places, lakes
never yet found...

Sod of birth,
sod of death,

ask me again
to eat the tree.

THE GOBÁN SAOR

Find the tap
that *elixir vitae*
may still be drawn,

open an ear
to his anvil's din,
name the colour
of every wind

or, particular night,
your prayers said,
divine his deepest well,

The Gobán Saor's
Grey White-Loined.

An almighty calm,
field, hills, world
one lambent pause:

she faces the way
you must go,

gather yourself,

your feet your fortune
on the shining grass.

THAT ONE

Felicity Wellbeloved
once said to me:
Deaf knows the songs,
Blind reads the stars,
Maimed wins the prize.
My lover is dead
by night, he lives
the livelong day.
His name's Nonpareil.
Ever search your grave?
I leap my tombstone
as you the daisy.

OCTOBER MORNING

Hussy vermilion rose-hip,
haw's *Beaujolais Nouveau*,

blackberry's puckered regret,
comether drowse of the sloe,

snowberry's clustered
pallor on pallor,

fistfuls of silence
where winter winds blow.

WHAT THE EGG SAID

There she is

on her nest
of bits and pieces —

You're most welcome.

Ripe for this
as you are loth,

her bloodied *pus*
sips the light.

TOCCATA

Today's *Irish Times*,
inside page, lower half,
offers a beautiful poem,

half page bare bar
this one poem, it
has all the space
in the wide world;

note, in that regard,
short lines galore —
you may extend these recklessly,

that's allowed since
here's no ordinary poem,
Compose as you read
is the chosen form,

by no means easy
but get accustomed
you'd have it no other way,

lines shape or melt,
shift, firm, alter,

all hangs on you,
on your eye, lips,
tongue, simple breath;

the yield is flux,
contained, adamant,
soft as a thigh,

and the poem's about?
it's about the colours
which famously embellish
The Book of Hours,

impertinent to quote
from such a poem,
Compose as you read
is no trivial pursuit

and yet — two lines,
two lines follow me,
won't let go,

lines such as these
must be spoken out,

I know the voice,
no one talks
the least like you,

there's no one meets
words quite your way,

who else would aver
to the faint of heart —

For a long time now I've
felt your lips on mine.

NOVEMBER

Now is the goose summer,

now a fine filmy substance
lifts from grassy surface
or from air descends
to deck the vagrant geese,
roly-poly mistresses of *clabar*:

this inexorable harmony
infuriates the gander
but abides —

on flight-paths of ochre,
lemon, flustered rosé,

small spiders ply
uninsurable looms.

REVERSE CHARGES

You should have known Eve,
the girl next door, fair
priestess of *vin ordinaire*,

or what about Helen?
patchouli of boudoir, poetry
talk, arc of her lingerie
a Calder mobile, *Helen,*
that was the rainy season,

I was born for Mary's
multiple assumptions, annunciations,
Mary, mine ethereal Mary,
come back Eve from Tipperary,

which brings us to Sophie,
Sophie, where are you?
and why don't you call?

oh, Eve on a journey,
Helen turned wise, Mary
down from the mountain,

I wait by the phone,

Sophie, please call. Call,
Sophie. Sophie, please call.

CHANGING HOUSE

Last chest, last drawer,
a lock of woman's hair.
Her very colour, sheen,
blonde brought up on sun.
Test the strands, brittle
something, sapless, stagey.
Smell, as you often did,
gulp now, gulp your fill.
Sandalwood of the drawer.

Look at it again,
light on your palm.

Finders —
Keepers —
Losers.

Soundlessly, the plastic bag
takes it in one go.

A L'AVENIR

A middle-aged man
measures the branches

while me bucko swans it
in the tree-top:
blackbird right shoulder,
left hand vessel of bronze,
trout in the vessel
plus bob of an apple,
butt of the tree
the stag who belongs

and miles away
the beautiful one
is thinking — *Today,*

*westerly, the wind
comes in lumps.*

She cups a hand
to catch the sea.

ARBOR VITAE

September you fed
on the living wood,

October that idol
grew from the bole,

you danced November
clothed in the branches,

watched with her
the longest time,

freed the prisoner
of hand-me-downs,

saw her ash-blonde
turn my red-gold,

knew I was home
and desired to be,

March the bridegroom
rode out of the tree.

BABY IN THE FIRE

Tickle an ear
he hops up and down
like an egg in a ponger,

I'm The Monsoon-Horse,
hums the clear of his eye,
I'm The Martinmas Gander,
I sleep like a thrush,
I don't look at calendars,
I'm your permanent bash
and The Patron of Hauliers.

Pause (mine) for breath.
The smile on offer's — earth-lit.

Look, he points, *Lookat —*

in the park opposite
a row of horse-chestnut
bursts into leaf,

There's foliage, Mister. If
it's foliage you're after.

Leaves of two colours
invite us, envelop us,

That child's a flamer,
sings the green, sings the yellow,

Make your shoulder his pillow,
sings the green, sings the yellow.

THE WHITE BIRD

The white bird hurls
herself against my window,

the pane shudders,
the bird rebounds.

A simple matter
to open the window,
bid the bird enter,

I know her aim
as she knows mine,
there are times
the aims intertwine,

our aims have been
occasionally at one,
these days we're driven
to sustain the word "then".

                *****

What is it
about her? Creature
of intolerable demands?
It isn't that, it's
her outspoken glance,
unruly tenderness
induces fear — quite
uncalled for, I know,

the silver birch
allowed her sun
and labile shade —
"You know too much" —
she took this in,
behold her eyes
limber all my joints,
"You've heard of a search
and engage mission?"
The branch sighed,
the compass spun, I
saw my wit's end
immaterialise
in wisps of cloud.

*****

Perdurable liaison.
Would you call us
lovers? Companions, as
they say nowadays?
Farouche Darby & Joan?
We boast a history
and that history boasts
mute abatement, heists,
Dear Johns, No more
Mister Nice Guys,
tearful *Je t'adore*,

I've seen her languish
under the stripped bush,
glutted, prostrate,

the flies thought
they had it made,
the flies who call
a spade a spade,

held her too
in my ambiguous arms,
quickly the *pas-de-deux*
gaped for nostrums,

nevertheless she was
once in my embrace.

*****

Hen-pheasant
embonpoint
on the lap of
an amiable Chinese,

back-to-the-wall dove,
chick on shoulder
as night stirred
the restive kerbstones,

the speckled bird
(butter wouldn't melt)
aloof in my garden,

Mistress Black Swan,
vid. supra, vid.infra,
ingest the scorch along
every lateral line,

versatile proprietaire
of chutzpah disguises,

your intricate repertoire,
my simpleton radar.

*****

I talk like a lover,
I make no move,

she will try again
and before long,
she isn't one
to dim intention,

is your scheme
haste-to-the-wedding
resuscitation?

Mouth-to-mouth
heroics, shots,
marvels of traction,
sutures, tourniquets,
drips, drops, in-
sufflations,

high contained
Hippocratic smile
as she revives,

convalescence
on the usual basis,
pick of the hedgerows,
tested spring water,
southern exposure,
volutes of laughter...

Thus, by slow degrees,
dulces et amabiles,
to the desideratum
of *vade mecum*.

*****

Long past that,
Mister ould Codger
fixing the ledger.

In the draughty zone
of one and one
just might make three,
button your coat

and from the bliss
of informed idleness
count the score :

plain as porpentine
there's death in the air,
glass in the pane,

glass between us
and all harm,

product of fusion
and instant cooling,

transparent, lustrous,
hard, amorphous,

possessed of nothing
if not insouciance,

supply — limitless,
dear second skin,
weather-eye within,

impetigo mine,
anchor of morning.

*****

Summer person, own
your summer occupation,

you sang all summer,
the grass was long,
the trees hung wide,
the bee-bread flowed,

you sang your song,
you call that doing,
you sang your summer,
now meet the other,

dance winter long
the winter dance,

you've sung your song,
you call that doing,
you've sung your song,
now dance the dance.

*****

It is the calmest
imaginable process,

the fire within
does all the work,

bits detatch themselves
haphazardly, tumble
careless through the grating,

the consenting adult
turns to ash

at a good steady pace,
there's no charge,

there's no survivor
bar the fire, our
insurmountable fire,

please sign here
if you're game
for the journey,
strip in the next room.

*****

I wander the floor
as day gathers,
step on to a balcony.
A quick silence,

the lake has just
slipped from the womb,

the banked evergreens
bless my father.

She flies close
to the still surface

on her approach
from the western end.

There are two birds,
the white bird
and her reflection

but singular the flight,
of clear intent,

there's no hurry,
there's no delay,

they come abreast
in dreamy saraband

and difficult to tell
which is bird,
which reflection,

they swop habiliments
a dozen times
before my question,

I go with that,

watch the pair
pronounce an hour,

pursue the course, absorb,
absorb the kindling haze.

THE SEA POTATO

My love brings
a sea potato, heart
urchin of the lower shore,
modestly sand-coloured
with soft backward-
pointing spines : no teeth,
she asserts, who has well
perused her *objet trouvé,*
the versatile spines pass food
to the pert mouth,
and, she is not slow
to point out the sea
potato is singularly petalled,
her pliant index finger
explores, reveals, five
dorsal petals, anterior
extending a sibilant
auxiliary mouthward groove —

Smell, she says: fume,
fume of salt furrows,

Listen, she says, places
against my ear the soft
sand-coloured thing:

arpeggio, silken, ten
thousand shells chime
in the wave's undertow.